THE UNCERTAINTY OF LOVE

Charleston, SC
www.PalmettoPublishing.com

The Uncertainty of Love
Copyright © 2023 by Antonio Amato

All rights reserved
No portion of this book may be reproduced, stored in a retrieval system, or transmitted in any form by any means–electronic, mechanical, photocopy, recording, or other–except for brief quotations in printed reviews, without prior permission of the author.

First Edition

Paperback ISBN: 979-8-8229-2181-8

ANTONIO AMATO

The Uncertainty of Love

LUST

LOSS

ANGER

AND

A REKINDLED SOUL

The First Time

Mass hysteria
Ultimate confusion
Insomnia
Sober disillusion

Breath after breath
Beat upon beat
Brow dripping
Thought obsolete

Rabid movement
No coordination
Quivering
Isolation

Interjecting feet
Highlighted fear
No ambition
Only I hear

Dreams
Previously dead
Awake and alive
Echoing in my head

Under The Sun

Everywhere you want to be
I must be the one
Whenever you look for me
I'll be everywhere under the sun

As far as the eye can see
Like a blooming flower sitting pretty
Covered by the shade of a tree
No where to run
I'm everywhere under the sun

Easy to find just open your eyes
I know it's been long, please don't apologize
I'm still waiting, waiting for you
Look into your heart, you'll know what to do

I'm already running, running to you
Like a speeding bullet or a passing train
I'm going to surround you like the pouring rain

Stripped me bare, come to me if you dare
You know I'm the one
I'm everywhere under the sun

You made me what I have become
Now I'm everywhere under the sun

A Gift From God

I love to watch you sleep, and I wonder while you breathe deep
Why you hang around a guy like me
When you grab my hand and place it next to your heart
I wonder what you see

A gentle kiss goodnight
A caress so soft and sweet
Makes butterflies in my stomach erupt
Every time we meet

We hold each other throughout the night, not letting go
I feel you, look at you…and I just know

I have received a gift from God that I must embrace
No dragon I must slay or struggles I may face
Will steal my attention from the one thing I cannot replace

I love to watch you sleep
And I wonder, while you breathe deep
Why you hang around a guy like me

Every Time I See Her

She ignores me when we are together
No phone calls when we are apart
Every time I see her
It's like an arrow through my heart

Sometimes, I think she doesn't know that I am alive
I give her all that I am
Every time I see her
She makes me feel like half a man

She treats me bad
Steps on my feelings, carves me up inside
Always unsure of myself, it's actually quite sad

The apple of my eye is rotten to the core
She's sweet, she's sour, she's cruel, she's kind
But day or night I don't mind
I couldn't love her more

She lives to bring me down
I'd die if she wasn't around
Every time I see her
My hands and knees are on the ground

My Girlfriend

She's high maintenance
With no repentance
A lack of substance
So, I try to keep my distance

Sometimes I would rather be alone than to deal with this
Forget about her divine lips and powerful kiss
Which I would hate to miss
But would sacrifice to avoid her kind of bliss

Nothing to talk about
Except when we fight
Then it's a heavyweight bout
Knocking me down, leaving me with no doubt
That she has the clout
To keep me from walking out

Her grip is strong
And it's been so long
That I don't know what is wrong

It took me months to get in
Which was the beginning of my downward spin
I was the balloon, she was the pin
All this time still living in sin

My Destiny

An epic story of my true love
Sent to me from the heavens above
We will climb atop the Acropolis
Look into each other's eyes and kiss
Lips locked
As we stand alone on this massive rock
For all to see that we were meant to be
And together we shall stay throughout all eternity

Thunder rolled like never before
And when the lightning struck down upon me
I knew what the God's had in store
My destiny revealed to me
More that I could ever dream for
I don't need a God's eye to see
That you are the one I will adore

As time continues to grow old
There is one thing left that needs to be told
For everything in the world that is sacred and true
You must remember, I've been placed on this earth
Because I am destined to love you

~

The Puppeteer

All that was needed was a little time
To hook up the strings that infiltrate your mind

You let her invade the space that was genuine and pure
Dirty the place that trust is no more

She plays the music that makes you dance
She allows nothing for second chance

The blindfold is tied and she can still see
How she knows what she knows is not a mystery

Turned your head and she jumped on your back
It took a second of your time
To hook up the strings that infiltrate your mind

She is a genius with her clothes off
That's the naked truth
The blood is on her hands
But he has no proof

She pulls the strings
That make him do these crazy things

The show goes on till you cut her loose
If you wait the strings will fit like a noose

Suffocate what's left, take your last free breath
Until then, she pulls the strings
And you deserve all it brings

Dirty Dog

You filter my thoughts
Words do not come out like I planned
The bone is in my mouth
And I await your command

Locked all the doors
Pulling the chain that keeps me on all fours

Obey the laws
Maybe, she will release your paws

I'll scratch your back if you lick mine
Do onto others, rule number sixty-nine

The more you struggle
The more she will tease
She may never stop
Even if I am begging please

My bark does not compare to her bite
I lay down, turn over and give up the fight

Something About Her

There is something about her I just can't describe
When she walks in the room, I feel so alive

Her smile is contagious
Her soul courageous

One look into her eyes
My world opens up
From the ocean to the clear blue skies

A kiss from her lips, a touch of her hand
Without her, I am half a man

She stole my heart like a thief in the night
With the moon shimmering and the stars shining bright
My head on the pillow as she holds me tight

There is something about her I just can't describe
Without her I would not want to be alive

In Love With An Angel

Tired and lonely, too many miles away
The minutes and hours seem longer than your average day
The summer month feels so cold
My body shivers with your absence and the night is too old
But I remember, you opened your wings and let me see
The passion, the love, I was blinded by your beauty

Now I cry
Don't need the comfort of a stranger to get me by
Grab my hand, teach me to fly
I want to share the clouds, I want to dance in the sky
I need your angel ways to show me why

I wake up alone
The morning is full of emptiness from the night before
I'm human again, because you are not with me anymore

Please don't leave me…as she takes flight
I don't want to sleep in this bed without your love tonight

Sweet Little Girl

The truth comes like a stranger
Unrecognized in front of your face
The lies fly from your mouth, but always full of grace

There are no exceptions in her school
Wrong is right when deception is the rule
My tongue is tied, yours is twisted
Words are meaningless, when my heart has just been lifted

I needed you to be my disguise
In this overgrown place I have learned to despise
But you seeped into this corrupt filled world
And I lost you forever, that sweet little girl

A diamond in the rough
Will cut you like glass when she thinks she has had enough
Her whispers scream inside my ringing head
As she pulls the plug and lays me down to bed
Does as she pleases and says what she believes
A great honor she stands a killer among thieves

Where were you when I needed you most
Vacant friendship passed through me like a ghost
Alone in this evil world
Where you are lost forever, my sweet little girl

Not You

A million and one promised to me
Like a politician in an election year
Everything I want to hear
But nothing I will ever see

The sun is peeking through the clouds
And I've been picking flowers for days
On Sunday paid a visit to your house
Only to find there is no water left in your vase

Forgiveness is free
This doesn't mean I give it away
If you are going to lie, think up something new
Not the one from yesterday

There is a picture moving in my head
It looks like you, but it's not
I know there was something I want to say
But I must have forgot
My wounds have yet to heal
I'm still waiting for my blood to clot

A million and one promised to me
Like a child waiting for the tooth fairy
I am not that naive
You can't believe everything you see
And see everything you believe

Built Up Dust

She's an open book for all to read
I'm a locked diary with just one key
She is a rage filled monster filled with jealousy
Blindfolded I can still see

I have finally opened my eyes to realize this immature obsession
So how do I break the silence and reveal this halfhearted confession

We have grown still and built up dust
With a fist as a hand we suffocate our trust
And sink to the bottom where we are left to rust

I promised to always be there
Now I think to myself, do I even care

A touch once so soft and sweet now forgotten
A look of love in a blur has disappeared
I no longer have the time to wait
For this loving feeling to reappear

Navel Lint

I'm so low I couldn't even make it into my high school band
I'm a rerun of a TV show you just couldn't stand
I'm the guy at the beach you want to bury in the sand

I'm the dictionary definition of a bum
I have no flavor, a dried-up piece of bubble gum
I'm navel lint, I'm slime, I'm lower than snail scum

I'm a wine stain on a new dress that won't come out
You are a headache, I am a kindergarten class that likes to scream and shout
I'm the biggest jerk on the face of the earth without a doubt

I'm sorry
I know you have heard it before
I'm sorry
I promise it won't happen anymore
Please forgive me
Before you walk out that door

Seasons Change

On the last page of the calendar
X marks the spot
Where my memories drifted away
Twas the season I forgot

Spending time with a stranger I have known for years
Awaken myself from sleeping with all of my fears
While the weather outside is frightful, I cry my dried-out tears

My once open heart has stiffened
With no presents left to see
All I want for Christmas
Is under someone else's tree

No spirit, no snow
No one to kiss under the mistletoe
The chimney is out of wood and I have no words left to say
The Grinch stole Christmas and replaced it with an ordinary day

Wasted Away

I knew it all along I just couldn't believe my own eyes
The disrespect, the betrayal, the lies

I'm so angry at myself for staying as long as I did, even when I knew the truth
All the signs were there, the text messages, the late nights, I had the proof

I wanted a lover and a friend
You wanted to create a family and pretend

Your heart was never true, at least not to me
Even you would have to agree

We used to have Tuesday nights under the covers
Then the excuses started to come, one after another

Fake smiles and meaningless conversation
Empty feelings and building frustration

Time just wasted away
Now there is literally nothing left to say

That's crazy after all these years I don't have one good memory to hold on to
Only a legacy of the pain that you put me through

Twenty-Two

I've reached that point in life
Where I have nothing left to give
I'm only twenty-two
No hopes or dreams
No plans or schemes
Where do I go, what do I do

I'm scared to fail in life
My biggest fear is creeping in
I'm lost somewhere in time
And I don't know where to begin

Amongst the confusion, there is more
Sacrifice, hard work, stay strong
What if I can't, what if they are wrong
What if I have been fooling myself all along

I have so little time left
To do the things I should want to do
So sad, I'm only twenty-two

The Sirens, The Lights

The sirens, the lights
The unknown faces that filled the night
Heaven's dogs are barking my way
The cold pavement is still, I can hear myself pray
A love gone mad is my sole possession
Defeated again by a past obsession

I blew it again
There is nothing left for me if she is not there
I was on top again
Life spins too fast, it's just not fair

My mind was turning I needed to clear my head
I drove to the Spot and hooked up with an old friend instead

I shouldn't have done it, after the first it was already too late
My emotions got the better of me, I just couldn't wait

I can't go on living
If she is not by my side
I had to tell her I love her
How I want her to be my bride

I drove off into the night racing down the street
It happened so fast I lost control
I could not see a thing, it was where the intersection meets

All I remember were the sirens the lights
And all of the unknown faces that filled the night

Goodnight To The King

Ignore the feelings in this place
All there is, just copy and paste

Visit the throne
Where he spends his time all alone

No power no command
Watch the blood drip from his wrinkled hand

Empty screams heard by all
Unglued pieces are ready to fall

Head turning teeth scratching
Body trembling everyone watching

Torn apart, the years have not been kind
Lost his heart now his mind

Sits in front of the window
Wrapped with his dusty cape
The sunlight hits his face
Blinding him through the drapes
He leans back and crashes on the cold wooden floor
Closes his eyes, he just can't take it anymore

Visions of the queen pass him by
As the choir begins to sing
The son sets over the castle
For a final goodnight to the King

Guttural Roar

I hurt in silence for a long time
No one knew, the pain was all mine

Days would continue to turn
And they would be surprised to learn

The darkness in me never subsides
It beats, it breathes, it does not hide

Every step was an uneasy one
No laughter, no fun

Fighting the thoughts in my head
My body lifeless in my bed

Wondering aloud with a guttural roar
A once promising life is no more

The Punches

They say roll with the punches
But the punches hurt
They have swelled up my eye
I can no longer see straight
Life's work has now made me late

The bills are unpaid
There is no food on the table
The children are crying
Is daddy unable

One to the gut
Two to the face
I have thrown up my hands
Waving the white flag in total disgrace

The punches are still coming
Day after day
The more they come
The more I want to roll away

Unopposed

Instead of melting from the sun
Or burning from the fire in its arm
It stood still in the wind and did no harm

The wind blew again and set it free
No conflict or struggle to be disposed
This is when I jumped out of my window
From the 13th floor, I want to be unopposed

Stress free ride from beginning to end
Swinging on the jungle gym with an old friend

My mind wanders endlessly
Free to reach its own conclusion
Imagine what it would be like
A world without confusion

Destiny unknown
No moss grows on a rolling stone
Continue to move all alone
Until I feel what I condone

I feel like fire
I feel like air
I feel like water
I am everywhere

Loneliness

I have turned the tide
To watch my enemy hide
Squirming away to the other side
I follow to take what's left of its pride
And give it one final ride

Stare me straight in the eye
As it began its retreat
The sounds of its pounding feet
Softer and softer, it fades away
Turn around, just fade away

Loneliness lurks, it's all I see
But for once its afraid, its afraid of me

The terror I bring to the fear that is no more
It took so much time to even the score
In your face when you least expect it
But you expect it all the time
Willing to punish for any and all crime
But not me, not anymore, this is the last time

Loneliness lurks, it's all I see
But for once its afraid, its afraid of me

Reborn

The anguish and the pain
All the suffering in vain
Grab me by the throat and drag me down
Offer me to this God forsaken town

My body battered, insides torn
I wish I was dead or better, not even born

I'm a shell of a man and I'm about to crack
The devil took me for a ride
Now I don't know how to get back

My body battered, insides torn
I wish I was dead or better, not even born

I lay still, blood on my clothes, blood on the ground
With my last breath I pray that somehow I will be found

My body battered, insides torn
I wish I was dead or better, never born

A warm hand reaches out, wipes the blood from my face
Picks me up and offers some space
I rise to the silhouette of my new best friend
Now I'm whole, I have what I need
Shamefully, it took me to the very end

My body battered, insides torn
I wish you were dead, or better, that you were never born

Stabbed

No reason for the action
No apology for the deed
I knew he was coming for me
As sure as I live and breathe

The fact remains
I'm bleeding, with my face to the floor
The sounds of his footsteps echo
As he walks out the door

I saw him pick up the knife
I felt him behind me
I took a deep breath, closed my eyes
Waited for him to stab me

Took me weeks to get the knife out of my back
Months to take it out of my heart
All these years to build
And one day to fall apart

It's In My Blood

I am my father's son
This I know for sure
Without prevention or cure

A bloody rage when things go wrong
A striking hand for that same old song

I lose my temper on the drop of a dime
On every occasion I swear it's my last time

I have been walking in his shoes my entire life
The same shoes that used to kick me down
I use to kick my son around

I see his face
And I see my own
It's in my blood
It's in my home

Without prevention or cure
I know for sure
I am my father's son

Elephant Song

Trapped between your legs
Thoughts uncontrolled in your head
As you surrender yourself to my head
Sweat filled body stuck to the bed
No reason or need to look ahead

Another number under the spell
Drowning in your own wishing well
Thinking back while walking away
Confined to me where you will stay

I am the elephant never forget
I am the elephant who gets you wet
I am the elephant never forget

You will fall to my domination
This is my game you are my creation
I am the master you are the slave
I know the poison which you crave
Absorb me, serve me like the king
Give up, I am your everything

I am the elephant never forget
I am the elephant who gets you wet
I am the elephant never forget

A lit up cigarette in her hand
As she is sprawled on the floor
Through the smoke I can see
Her hungry eyes begging for more

Last Night

I put on my favorite shirt
And my brand new shoes
For a night on the town
To chase away my blues

A couple of drinks and I'm feeling good
When I looked at the bar and there she stood

Two friends and a wine glass by her side
She looked at me, I stared at her, it just felt right

We didn't even make it to the bedroom door
Stumbled into the apartment with urgency on the living room floor

Making love wherever and whenever
If only this night could last forever

Then the morning came and she woke up alone
WIth a rose on her pillow and a note by her phone

Last night was great but I'm a married man
No hard feelings, I hope you understand

Me and My Phone

Sunrises and sunsets, beautiful flowers, that special look in someone's eye
These are things I currently don't see
Holding hands, a comforting hug, for the longest time I used to wonder
Why can't it be me

I wake up and stare at my phone
Everyone is so happy, going places, living their lives
I'm in my bedroom all alone

At work or at parties everyone shares stories, I have nothing to say
Late nights, long weekends, trips across the globe
I'm home wondering why does no one want to stay

Then the night comes, I try and go out on a date or two
Some are promising some are one and done
Some even get me excited and I begin to have fun

Then the cycle repeats
I wake up and scroll through my phone
Watching everyone else be happy
And me, still all alone

When are things going to change
What do I need to do
Being lonely is more difficult than I thought
Might be the hardest thing I have ever been through

Every morning and every night
Looking at my phone as my saving grace
And the cycle repeats
I always wake up in the same exact place

All alone
Stuck in my head
No one
Just me and my phone in bed

No More Fear

Thoughts and visions twirl around my head,
 by my side, all around

I close my eyes and the darkness hits me without a sound

Do I listen to my head or my heart
or do I wait until I'm completely torn apart

Confused unsettled undecided misguided

My body shouts so loud that it drowns out the world behind

Now it's a straight line to the one I need to find

She's been there all along singing in my ear
Hold on so tight, no more fear

And Then I Met You

I don't like rom-coms, or watch reality TV shows
I don't get overly excited during the highs, or too sad during the lows

I don't believe in cliches or happy endings
I don't feel the need to lie and I'm not into games or pretending

And then I met you
I lose track of time I don't know the day
Nothing else in the world seems to matter
And I like feeling this way

I don't like candlelight dinners
I don't like slow love songs that you can dance to
I don't want to go hiking or walk on the beach
It's all the same even the view

I don't like staying in on Sunday morning
Having brunch in the newest trendy spot
Sometimes I don't want to get up at all
I feel like the man that the world simply forgot

And then I met you
You make me feel like I fit
You make all the wrongs seem right
Everyday and every single night

And then I met you
My cup is half full, not empty
My life has meaning now
I finally feel like the man I was always meant to be

Distracted

The thought of you was swimming in my head before we met
The sight of you I won't soon forget
Your hair, MMM your smell
I think we were talking, but I can't tell

I'm distracted

Our eyes lock, the night feels new
I want to be calm, but I know I am not…what do I do

I'm distracted

Then that smile buckled my knees
Whatever I'm feeling, I want more please

Distract me
With lips I can kiss til the end of time
Distract me
With a love so pure I can call mine

The Lighter

I have so many words in my head and in my heart
The pen is in my hand I just don't know where to start.

Maybe I'm just waiting for my muse
Someone to truly open my eyes and light the fuse

All the years of neglect have built up a wall
Then I think of you and piece by piece it begins to fall

You see me

With a look, a touch or just a smile
I'm happily lost for a long long while

You feel me

All the colors are brighter the days and nights seem longer
My heart my mind my body, feel stronger

You thrill me

My fingers, my breath,
My lips, my everything
Every ounce of me, wants for you
Every thought and desire, is you
You light me up
I'm on fire

I Can't Explain

I had other plans the night we met
One look at you and I can't explain
Everyone else I would soon forget

That first night everything went right
The sound of the rain
Background music for my brain

Sitting across from you
Hearing you laugh, seeing you smile
Feeling hopelessly trapped in your sweet sexy style

The caress of your hand, that first kiss
Knowing with certainty I have never had a feeling quite like this

A pitcher of beer, a bottle of wine
Closing down the bar again every single time

Morning texts, good night calls
An afternoon distraction
With every word my insecurities fall

My hand on your face
The comfort of your embrace
The happiness I feel to find a strand of your hair on the pillowcase

Every moment seems better than the one before
And I can't explain it but my God I want more

Over and Over

You were just a picture
A text message, a call
Now eyes wide open
I don't want a piece I want it all

I want to call you baby
I want to hear you say my name
This is as real as it gets no more games

The car
The apartment door
The couch, the kitchen table
The bathroom floor

This connection has taken over
We have lost all control
No thinking
Two bodies two souls

I have a never-ending taste for you
Your body begins to shake, this is only the beginning
And we're not close to being through

We smile as we catch our breath
It's almost all we can take
Then one look and we can't resist
Diving back in with passion you just can't fake

Over and over
Free to explore
My fantasy turned reality
Complete and undeniable this woman I must adore

Being With You

Morning coffee is gonna have to wait
Work will be late
The one thing on my mind is lying beside me, looking so sweet
I need to take my time
Working my way, down to your feet

Our fingers unlock as the sunlight breaks
A playful kiss on the cheek anticipating your return
Trying to move forward
As my insides burn

The clock seems to be on pause
Time moves slowly and I think about all our imperfections and all our flaws
But our past mistakes mean nothing when we're together
I push your button you pull my lever

Reliving the images of last night
Biting the inside of your arm,
Legs wrapped around me so tight
Trusting each other to do no harm

What I'm feeling must only happen to a lucky few
Everyone talks about going to heaven
But I can't imagine a place better than being with you

Gray Sweatpants

A lot of men claim to be the luckiest man alive
I don't care about them, they're all wrong
I know it's me as I sit here writing another love song

I'm continually amazed by you
Whether we are out with friends or home cooking dinner, laughing as we slow dance
Whether you're in that little black dress or on the couch with those gray sweatpants

There are not enough words to describe how beautiful you are
You shine greater than the brightest star
You knock me off of my feet without even trying
I need you to believe me you are that damn good baby, I'm not lying

You level me with a look across the room
You leave me no chance
Addicted to you, whether you are in that little black dress
Or those gray sweatpants

Late nights losing sleep always worth it
You are the one that I just can't quit
Every night feels so new
A little kiss, a passing touch
It is every single thing you do
Makes me want you so much

My head spinning, our friends are jealous of this whirlwind romance
So completely into you, whether you're in that little black dress or those gray sweatpants

I Have Your Back

No matter where you are
Or what you do
You and me are unconditional
Just know I got you

One thousand percent
I have your back
That is the truth
A concrete fact

Anytime day or night
The gloves are off I'm in for the fight

Even when you are wrong
We may get hurt and we may bleed
I will not hesitate
I will be everything you need

No words need to be spoken
Always all in
My word and my bond will not be broken

If you need my shoulder
I will listen to you cry
If you want to run and hide
I will not ask you why

One thousand percent
I have your back
That is the truth
A concrete fact

www.ingramcontent.com/pod-product-compliance
Lightning Source LLC
LaVergne TN
LVHW051925060526
838201LV00062B/4682